# CONNECTING THROUGH COMMUNICATION

### THE ART AND SCIENCE OF CREATING EMOTIONALLY INTELLIGENT, GENUINE CONVERSATIONS

## COLIN CHRISTOPHER

**Course Companion**
**Second Edition**

This book belongs to:

Name: _____

Mailing Address: _____

City or Town: _____

State/Province: _____

Zip/Postal Code: _____

Telephone: _____

Training Date: _____

CONNECTING THROUGH COMMUNICATION
The Art and Science of Creating
Emotionally Intelligent, Genuine Conversations

Course Companion

Second Edition

Colin Christopher

Published by
Manchester House Publishing
www.manchesterhousepublishing.com

The author of this book does not dispense medical advice or prescribe the use of any technique as a form of treatment for physical, emotional, mental, spiritual or medical problems without the advice of a physician, either directly or indirectly. The intent of the author is only to offer information of a general nature to help you in your quest for physical, mental, emotional and spiritual wellbeing. In the event you use any of the information in this book for yourself, which is your right, the author and the publisher assume no responsibility for your actions.

ISBN: 978-1-9991335-1-1

Credits - 20210315

Jacket and Book design by Chris Simon
www.hotspotcreative.ca

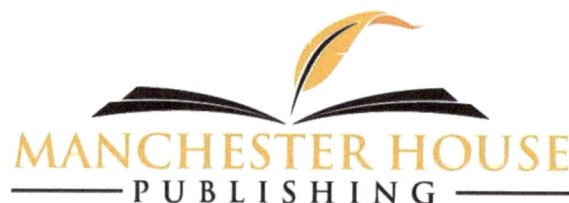

MANCHESTER HOUSE
— PUBLISHING —

# CONNECTING THROUGH COMMUNICATION
## THE ART AND SCIENCE OF CREATING EMOTIONALLY INTELLIGENT, GENUINE CONVERSATIONS

Connecting Through Communication helps you talk to the conscious and subconscious minds of the people you interact with. These psychological tools have been distilled into a tested, real world, easy to use system of conversation. As you learn the art and science of communication, you will be able to have comfortable, safe and trusting conversations, so you can:

✔ Use your F*****G mouth
✔ Bridge the communication divide between generations like Millennials and Boomers
✔ Provide space for listening, understanding, and reciprocation
✔ Identify and eliminate barriers to communication
✔ Resolve conflict with the power of your words
✔ Own the conversation
✔ Ask questions and respond in safe and effective ways
✔ Create meaningful, useful connections

| COMFORT | SAFETY | TRUST |
|---------|--------|-------|

## Interactive Online Training

Colin Christopher discuses and provides Psychological Tools based on Hypnosis, NLP, Neuroscience, and other Social Engineering techniques designed to help you communicate effectively. You will learn the skills to be confident and emotionally aware - so you have genuine conversations with anyone. You will learn to easily create comfort, safety, and trust in the minds of the people you talk to, so you have the pleasure of enjoying excellent, meaningful connections.

**www.ConnectingThroughCommunication.com**

# *What People Are Saying…*

*"Colin delivered an outstanding presentation to 25 of our Advisors. He received rave reviews from across the board with one of our most experienced Advisors stating, 'That was one of the best presentations I have seen in over 30 years in the business!' Thank you Colin!"*

**Greg Bird**

*"I was able to identify and pinpoint the differences between someone who just 'thinks positively' and someone who truly has mastered their thoughts and has them under control and therefore can produce results. I just wanted you to know that the way that you explained everything, and the organization of how it was put together is immaculate."*

**Victoria Luttman**

*"I have known Colin for a year now and he truly is a remarkable person. I have attended his class and was amazed at his style of teaching. His interactive approach was really helpful. Colin actually talks to you. He's genuine in his desire to help those that need his coaching. It's not what I thought his class was going to be, it was better. I would recommend his training to anyone. Thank you Colin. You are awesome!☺"*

**Trina Christensen**

*"I really appreciate his patience and explanations as we worked through the questions in real time. This was a fantastic seminar and if you get a chance to see him in person or online, I highly recommend it!"*

**Amber Brucker**

# *What People Are Saying... Continued...*

*"I just want to say that after taking the Colin Christopher courses, they really made a big difference in my business. One particular area that I have applied to my business and myself is Training the Gatekeeper (the mind). I used to be so scared to make calls – I would assume the result of the call before I even made the call.*

*Applying the training that Colin had given us, I was able to free myself of pre-conceived notions by training my mind to believe positive things and expect good results. Also, his courses reminded me not to take anything personal in sales calls. If I got an objection, I used to just cave in and proceed to end the call, but after the sessions, and also the one on one session, I am now able to further ask more probing questions without being too pushy.*

*I apply this same principle in networking situations as well, I try to ask questions about the individual I'm speaking with in order to steer that conversation in the way I want it to go. Due to applying what I have learnt, I was able to win the CIBC Quarterly Achievers Award for Q32017...Thanks Colin...You're the best :)"*

**Fiona Dwyer**

*"Very thorough and very passionate about his work! Well worth the time!"*

**Gary Johnson**

*"Colin is awesome and entertaining! I highly recommend him!"*

**Alannah Zilkowsky**

# What People Are Saying… Continued…

*"Colin is an excellent speaker and laid out the learning plan in a way that was easy to follow and understand. I believe the lessons I learned will help me move forward successfully in business, and recommend anyone to check him out. Thank you, Colin!!"*

**Louise Hogg**

*"I like how he incorporates mindset & psychology in his trainings."*

**Chantelle Christensen**

*"I have attended a couple of session with Colin and the information and work Colin presents is great and has helped me in my business. Thanks Colin"*

**Jeff Prediger**

*"The out-of-the-box, almost backwards way of looking internally and examining the way one act externally to influence more effectively is a welcome breath of fresh air from the high-pressure tactics and situationally focused material in popular coaching.*

*I would recommend the training programs to both B2B and B2C sales teams looking to improve service at the same time as sales."*

**Austen Knopp**

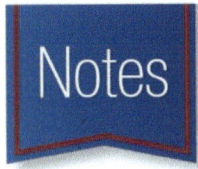

Connecting Through Communication
The Art And Science Of Creating Emotionally
Intelligent, Genuine Conversations

Notes

© Colin Christopher
www.ConnectingThroughCommunication.com

Connecting Through Communication
The Art And Science Of Creating Emotionally
Intelligent, Genuine Conversations

Notes

© Colin Christopher
www.ConnectingThroughCommunication.com

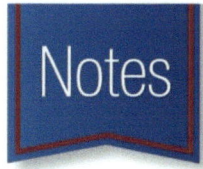

Connecting Through Communication
The Art And Science Of Creating Emotionally
Intelligent, Genuine Conversations

Notes

© Colin Christopher
www.ConnectingThroughCommunication.com

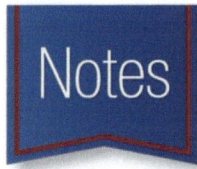

Connecting Through Communication
The Art And Science Of Creating Emotionally
Intelligent, Genuine Conversations

Notes

© Colin Christopher
www.ConnectingThroughCommunication.com

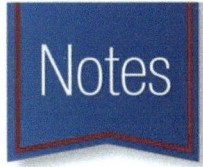

Connecting Through Communication
The Art And Science Of Creating Emotionally
Intelligent, Genuine Conversations

Notes

© Colin Christopher
www.ConnectingThroughCommunication.com

# Table of Contents

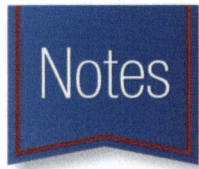

Connecting Through Communication
The Art And Science Of Creating Emotionally
Intelligent, Genuine Conversations

Notes

© Colin Christopher
www.ConnectingThroughCommunication.com

# *Week 1: Introduction*

1. What is Connecting Through Communication?

_____

_____

_____

_____

2. What is a thinking habit?

_____

_____

_____

_____

Notes

3. What are the 7 steps in the communication formula?

1. _____

2. _____

3. _____

4. _____

5. _____

6. _____

7. _____

4. What is conventional thinking?

_____

_____

_____

_____

5. What is unconventional thinking?

_____

_____

_____

_____

_____

6. What are the laws of manipulation?

_____

_____

_____

_____

7. What is the law of subconscious habits?

_____

_____

_____

_____

_____

8. What is the law of conscious interpretation?

_____

_____

_____

_____

9. What is the law of the gatekeeper?

_____

_____

_____

_____

_____

Complete the following exercises over the coming week.

Exercises:

1. Meditation
2. Hypnosis

# Exercise 1: Meditation

1. The focus of this exercise is to relax the gatekeeper of your conscious mind. You're doing this so you can begin to learn to influence your own subconscious thoughts.

2. Focus on your breath and let any thoughts you have go. If you want, you can have soft music with no lyrics playing in the background. Also, remember to set an alarm to remind you when you're finished.

3. Begin by doing meditation for 5 minutes and work up to 30 minutes.

4. Sit comfortably in a place where you will be uninterrupted and follow these 4 phases of breathing:

    i. Breathe in for 4 seconds.
    ii. Hold your breath for 4 seconds.
    iii. Breathe out for 4 seconds.
    iv. Keep your lungs empty for 4 seconds.

5. Start at 4 seconds for each phase above, and work your way up to 8 seconds (or longer if you can).

Notes

6. If you have difficulty holding your breath with your lungs full, or your lungs empty, then shorten the time back to 4 seconds (or less if needed). You want to focus on breathing, but you don't want to make it difficult for yourself either.

## Notes

## *Exercise 2: Hypnosis*

1. The focus of this exercise is to relax the gatekeeper of your conscious mind using hypnosis. Hypnosis is one of the most effective and fastest ways to bypass your gatekeeper.

2. The link to the free hypnosis recording for relaxation is at http://www.hypnosishealthstore.com. This hypnosis in not like on stage or TV. You're not going to be doing wild, crazy things – It's going to help your mind and body feel relaxed and reduce stress.

3. Listen to the recording 2 or 3 times over the coming week. Listen to it uninterrupted. You can do it before bed if you like, or during the day if you want to stay alert. That's up to you.

# Week 2: Planning And Eliminating Communication Anxiety

1. What is the law of language translation?

_____

_____

_____

_____

2. What is the law of opposite language?

_____

_____

_____

_____

Connecting Through Communication
The Art And Science Of Creating Emotionally Intelligent, Genuine Conversations

3. What is the law of triggers?

_____

_____

_____

_____

_____

4. Thinking about your communication skills, what do you feel triggers you in good or bad ways?

_____

_____

_____

_____

5. What is the law of association?

_____

_____

_____

_____

6. What is the law of fight or flight?

_____

_____

_____

_____

7. What are the symptoms of fight or flight?

_____

_____

_____

_____

_____

8. What triggers fight or flight – especially in communication scenarios?

_____

_____

_____

_____

Notes

Complete the following exercises over the coming week.

Exercises:

3. Identify and Eliminate Mental Barriers
4. Approach Strangers And Give Them A Compliment
5. Make Small Talk

# Exercise 3: Identify And Eliminate Mental Barriers

Answer the following:

Regarding meeting new people, or talking to co-workers, clients and friends/family:

1. Describe the situation that aggravates you the most. For example: Are you afraid of talking to someone new? What types of communication anxiety happen to you? Or is there something else that aggravates you?

_____

_____

_____

_____

_____

_____

Notes

2. Describe the DISADVANTAGES of this situation and what you RESENT the most about it. What do you feel this distress is keeping you from experiencing? For example: It keeps me from successfully expressing myself and makes me feel like I'm not living up to my potential or not getting my point across.

_____

_____

_____

_____

_____

_____

_____

3. Describe the situation you would like the pleasure of experiencing in the future, related to what aggravates you the most. For example: I would love to be able to walk into any networking event and easily talk to everyone very easily and comfortably.

_____

_____

_____

_____

_____

_____

_____

4. On a scale from 1 to 7, with 7 being the highest, how successful have you been so far towards reaching that experience?

_____

5. Describe what you like best about meeting new people.

_____

_____

_____

_____

_____

6. Describe the advantages to you of meeting new people.

_____

_____

_____

_____

7. Describe what you appreciate most about other people.

_____

_____

_____

_____

8. Describe how it feels for you to help other people.

_____

_____

_____

_____

9. Describe the best communication you've ever had with someone you've met for the first time. What did you talk about? Did you help them in some way, or did they help you in some way? How did they feel? How did you feel?

_____

_____

_____

_____

10. So far you've identified advantages, disadvantages, appreciations and resentments. With this accomplished, you want to start beating communication anxiety. Anxiety comes from focusing on disadvantages and resentment. It's time to change your focus. It's time to harness the power of focusing on advantage and appreciation. Review your answers to the previous questions and write out an affirmation tailored for your success. An affirmation you can focus on and repeat to yourself before you meet new people or talk to people you already know.

Use the following format:

I am comfortable, honest and trustworthy.

This makes me feel

_____,

because I offer

_____,

that helps

_____

feel

_____!

For example: I feel comfortable, honest and trustworthy. This makes me feel excited and grateful because I offer great conversation that helps the people I talk to feel comfortable and have fun!

Write your affirmation here:

_____

_____

_____

_____

The next 2 exercises are designed to help you start eliminating your communication anxiety by practicing. The idea is to shift your focus so that you are thinking about the affirmation you made in the first exercise combined with a focus on being comfortable, safe and trustworthy.

Before you start each exercise, either listen to the hypnosis recording that you were given or take 5 to 15 minutes to relax with meditation. You want to relax your gatekeeper so it's easier to concentrate your thoughts and shift into your new focus.

# Exercise 4: Approach Strangers And Give Them A Compliment

1. Go somewhere public, like a mall, coffee shop, anywhere there are lots of people you can meet. Even walking down the street.

2. Mentally state your affirmation from the first exercise or state the following affirmation: "I feel comfortable, honest and trustworthy. This makes me feel excited and grateful because I offer great conversation that helps the people I talk to feel comfortable and have fun!"

3. As soon as you look at a person, silently count to 3, move towards them and take a breath. As you breathe out, compliment that person about anything. You can say: "That's a great purse!" or "Awesome truck!" Any kind of compliment. It doesn't matter who you compliment. You're going out and being friendly and fun. You're training yourself to talk to someone within 3 seconds of seeing him or her, while maintaining your focus on being comfortable, honest and trustworthy in a real life scenario. This way you can stay calm.

Notes

4. You've succeeded once you've made the compliment. If any conversation proceeds that's a bonus.

5. Repeat this 5 times remembering to start with your affirmation. 10 or more is better if you have the time.

## Exercise 5: Make Small Talk

1. Go somewhere public, like a mall, coffee shop, anywhere there are people you can meet.

2. Mentally state your affirmation from the first exercise or state the following affirmation: "I feel comfortable, honest and trustworthy. This makes me feel excited and grateful because I offer great conversation that helps the people I talk to feel comfortable and have fun!"

3. Start a conversation with a stranger. As soon as you see them, silently count to 3, take a breath and ask them a question. The topic doesn't matter. You can talk about elections, the weather, the latest things happening in the news. For example you can say: "What do you think of the weather we're having?" or "Who do you think will win the hockey game tomorrow?" Basically any kind of question on a general topic where they can voice their opinion to you and vice versa. It doesn't matter whom you talk to. You're out to be friendly and fun. Just like in exercise 4 earlier, you're training yourself to talk to someone

Notes

within 3 seconds of seeing them and maintaining your focus on being comfortable, honest and trustworthy when you're in a real life communication scenario – so you can stay calm. You're also adding another layer of communication by learning how to ask comfortable questions to start and steer a conversation.

4. You've succeeded once you've made small talk. If any conversation proceeds beyond that, it's a bonus.

5. Repeat this at least 5 times starting with your affirmation.

# Week 3: Practice And Communication Starter Exercises

1. What is the law of repetition?

_____

_____

_____

_____

2. What is the law of concentrated attention?

_____

_____

_____

_____

3.  What is the law of dominant belief?

_____

_____

_____

_____

4.  What are the 3 ways to approach someone?

_____

_____

_____

_____

Complete the following exercises over the coming week.

Exercises:

6. Identifying Your Dominant Beliefs
7. Approaching In A Safe Way
8. Starting A Conversation

# Exercise 6: Identifying Your Dominant Beliefs

Answer the following:

1. Regarding your work over the last 2 weeks, how many times have you had a good day? When you're having a good day – what do you say, think, and/or repeat to yourself? What about in your personal life? Does feeling positive outside of work influence your day?

_____

_____

_____

_____

_____

_____

2. Regarding your work over the last 2 weeks, how many times have you had a bad day? When you're having a bad day – what do you say, think, and/or repeat to yourself? What about in your personal life? Does feeling negative outside of work influence your day?

_____

_____

_____

_____

_____

_____

_____

_____

_____

Notes

3. Comparing what you say/think/repeat to yourself, and the feelings this creates, describe your results. What are you concentrating on the most? How is this affecting your work? How does "what you concentrate on" affect your personal life?

_____

_____

_____

_____

_____

_____

_____

4. Examining how you feel – combined with what you say/think/repeat to yourself and your results above, think back to the affirmation you made at the end of *Exercise 3: Identifying and Eliminating Mental Barriers*. Do you feel the affirmation is strong enough to break through any negative thoughts and feelings you concentrate on? If they're positive, do you feel the affirmation supports your positive thoughts and feelings, or can the affirmation be improved? If you need to, adjust your affirmations according to what you feel will work best for you. If you need to, go through all of *Exercise 3* again and adjust your affirmation, or make a better one.

_____

_____

_____

_____

_____

_____

Notes

The next 2 exercises are designed for you to practice how to help people feel comfortable when you start a conversation. These are to be practiced in non-critical scenarios where your sales will not be affected. That way you can learn the skill and apply it to your sales as you progress. The idea is to remove or minimize subconscious perceptions that trigger the fight or flight response in the people you meet.

## Exercise 7: Approaching In A Safe Way

1. Go somewhere public, like a mall or anywhere there are lots of people you can meet. Even walking down the street. You're going to need space to walk towards people, so it has to be somewhere where you can walk at least 5 or 6 steps.

2. Mentally state your affirmation or use the following affirmation: "I feel comfortable, honest and trustworthy. This makes me feel excited and grateful because I offer great conversation that helps the people I talk to feel comfortable and have fun!"

3. As soon as you see someone that you can walk over to, silently count to 3, take a breath and walk over to them by approaching at an angle. Say "Hello" with a smile on your face. And keep walking. You're training yourself to walk over to someone at an angle, in a way that makes them feel safe.

4. Approach at least 10 different people at an angle and observe how they react when you say "Hello." Remember to repeat your

affirmation to yourself each time before you walk over.

5. You've succeeded once you've approached 10 people at an angle. If any conversation proceeds that's a bonus.

6. This last step is optional: If you want to see the difference in how people react – approach 5 people head on, and approach 5 people from behind (by tapping them on the shoulder). When doing these 2 types of approaches, give them a compliment like you did in *Exercise 4: Approach Strangers and Give Them A Compliment*. There has to be a reason to tap someone on the shoulder, otherwise you will make them feel very uncomfortable.

## Exercise 8: Starting A Conversation

1. Memorize the following communication starter:

   - Hey real quick, I'm heading across town right away to meet my next client, but let me get your take on something…
   - If you were to get a gift, would you rather it be a little too small, or a little too big?
   - The reason I'm asking is because it's my friends' daughter's birthday and I'm thinking of ordering her a custom T-Shirt from the Internet. For some clothes she wears a medium, and some she wears a large. I want her to feel good about wearing it. What do you think?

2. Go somewhere public, like a mall, coffee shop, anywhere there are people you can meet.

3. Mentally state your affirmation or use the following affirmation: "I feel comfortable, honest and trustworthy. This makes me feel excited and grateful because I offer great

conversation that helps the people I talk to feel comfortable and have fun!"

4. As soon as you see someone to talk to, silently count to 3, and walk over at an angle, take a breath and say the communication starter you memorized in step 1. It doesn't matter whom you talk to. You're having fun meeting people. You're training yourself to start a conversation in an interesting way while maintaining your focus on being comfortable, honest and trustworthy.

5. You've succeeded once you've gotten their opinion and shared yours with them. If any conversation proceeds beyond that, it's a bonus.

6. Repeat this at least 5 times starting with your affirmation and ending your conversation with "It was a pleasure meeting you. Thank you for your help! This way they feel appreciated.

## Notes on starting communication:

This communication starter does the following:

I. They're comfortable because you walked up at an angle.

Notes

II. You've alleviated any anxiety they might have of you taking up their time – because you set a time limit.

III. You've set a scenario where they can follow up about your occupation because you said you have clients. As conversation continues you've created a space where it's natural for them to ask about what you do.

IV. You've established that you're generous and think of people's feelings because you're buying someone a gift and you're conscientious about how they will feel when they receive it.

Depending on where you're meeting people, there are situations where time limits aren't needed. If you're at a networking event, or meet up group, or BNI, etc. – people are expecting you to talk to them. So instead you can start a conversation with a phrase like: "I love this event! I'm meeting some amazing people. Hey, let me get your take on something:" And then go into asking the question.

For memorizing, the easiest way is to read it out loud over and over again for 10 minutes. Keep repeating it until you're sure you have it memorized, you feel comfortable saying it, and it sounds like natural conversation. Always say it out loud as you memorize so you can hear how you're saying it and adjust your tone.

Memorize to be sure of the words. Be in a position where you don't have to think about what you're going to say when you start the conversation. That way you can focus on the people you're meeting instead of fumbling for things to say.

The question component of the communication starter is always the most important part and has to be memorized word for word. This is because if you say it wrong: They feel uncomfortable. It feels like you're being fake and that creates distrust.

The rest of the details of the question are easier to fill in. People sometimes ask about sending a gift card or getting a gift receipt and you can say you're shipping it, or you want it to be right the first time she puts the T-shirt on. The details aren't that important. Only that you ask the question correctly so they feel comfortable and respond to you.

This way you can get their opinion to start the communication. Once you have their opinion, give your position on what you think about sending the gift. Or after their opinion, tell them what you decided to do based on their input, and thank them for helping you.

If you happen to be talking to a group, get everyone's opinion before offering yours. Once you've shared opinions with everyone, the communication starter is finished. From here, if you want, you can continue the conversation, or you can leave after thanking them. Right now you're only practicing the communication starters so it's ok to end the conversation politely.

As you practice this and master the skill, the best communication starters will be based on your current experiences so you're telling the truth. When you're truthful – you're trustworthy – and that will come across when you're using these techniques.

But for right now, you're going to use this communication starter because it's been tested and works well so you can master and understand the skill. Once you've mastered the skill you can begin creating your own communication starters.

# Week 4: Interaction

What is the law of pressure proofing?

_____

_____

_____

_____

Complete the following exercises over the coming week. These exercises are designed for you to practice the very important skills of establishing comfort, safety, and trust with the people you meet, and recognizing whether they are in rapport with you. These are to be practiced in non-critical scenarios so you can learn the skill. The idea is to add skills incrementally to pressure proof your ability, use the skills effectively, and achieve peak performance.

Exercises:

9.  Tone And Speed Of Speech
10. Indicators Of Rapport
11. Creating Your Own Communication Starters
12. Bridging In The Right Direction

# Exercise 9: Tone And Speed Of Speech

1. Take an hour and watch some popular comedians on TV or YouTube or on Comedy Central at www.cc.com. As you watch, pay attention to how the comedians deliver what they are saying. Notice how they pace their speech: notice how they slow down and speed up, and notice the audience reactions as they do. Listen to the tone of their voice and pay attention to the tones you feel you trust more. Usually, the lower slower toned voices feel trust worthier.

2. Take a random book or news article (content does not matter), and record yourself doing the following:

    i. Read a page out loud in your normal voice.

    ii. Read the next page out loud but twice as fast.

    iii. Read the next page out loud but do it 25 – 50% slower in a lower tone of voice. Lower tone means – lowering your voice a little bit more than usual, yet still feels natural for you as you speak.

iv. Read the next page out loud again in a low tone, but read each sentence at different speeds and smile as you read. Smile comfortably with your eyes and whole face not just your mouth.

v. Listen to the recordings and observe how changing your speech changes your perception of yourself.

vi. Have 3 to 5 people listen to the recordings and when they're finished listening; ask them which tone and speed felt the most comfortable and trusting to them, as they listened.

# Exercise 10: Indicators Of Rapport

The purpose of this exercise is for you to learn to identify and determine when people are in and out of rapport.

1. Go somewhere public, like a mall or anywhere there are lots of people you can observe. Coffee shops and restaurants are excellent for this.

2. Take an hour and discreetly observe people and pay attention to how they interact. Specifically, look at couples, people on a business meeting, friends, and service staff. As you observe, notice their body language and tone of voice (if you can hear them – be inconspicuous). Look for the indicators of rapport between the people you observe. Also look for the indicators that show you these people are out of rapport with each other.

3. As you observe, identify at least 3 indicators of rapport to confirm your observations. 1 or 2 indicators may be enough in some circumstances, but the more indicators you see, the more valid your observations

become – especially if there are also indicators of non-rapport.

## Indicators of Rapport

1) They maintain solid eye contact.
2) Concern about appearance – they adjust their hair, smooth out or fix their clothes, or play with the buttons of their shirt or jacket.
3) They straighten their posture as if to pay attention.
4) They lean towards the person they're talking to – this can be a slight lean, or a larger one – but not swaying.
5) They can touch their face more than what seems usual.
6) If they have a glass or cutlery in their hands, they start playing with it by moving it back and forth or rolling it around.
7) Their lips, eyes and even nostrils open/flare as they listen to the speaker. Their brow may even rise. Their face is physically opening up and trying to take in everything being said.
8) Sometimes they might stutter slightly as they speak. This can indicate they're interested and concerned about what a person thinks and are nervous about how they are perceived.

9) They physically move closer to the person they're talking to and may even turn their body towards them. Their feet are the best indicator here. Their body may be facing the person, but if their feet are faced away, they are not connecting.

10) They tilt their head in one direction as they listen.

11) They touch the other person on the arm, elbow, or hand lightly. This is more common for women than men, but men will do it too.

12) They start asking questions without prompting. The conversation is not one sided.

13) They change their opinion on something based on the opinion of the other person.

14) They laugh at bad jokes, even if no one else is laughing.

15) They focus on one individual and ignore other people in the group that try to contribute to the conversation.

16) They mirror the body position, speech or tone of the person they're talking to.

## Non-Rapport Indicators

1) Their body is turned away, or they're leaning away/swaying back and forth from the person they're talking to.

2) They look annoyed / bored / disturbed / frightened.

3) Their feet are turned away from the person they're talking to.

4) They take steps back or away from the person they're talking to.

5) They squint as they're looking at the person they're talking to. They don't seem open to what's being said.

6) They're looking around instead of paying attention to the person they're talking to.

7) They repeatedly correct the person they're talking to, or offer their opinions that are contrary. It's almost like they're disagreeing on purpose to pick a fight.

8) They seem out of sync with the person they're talking to – they're not mirroring.

9) They quickly try to change subjects, or talk about how they have to leave right away, or abruptly end the conversation, or they leave at a non-natural point in the conversation.

10) They're more interested in talking to other people.

# Exercise 11: Creating Your Own Communication Starters

Keeping the following items in mind, its time to create your own communication starter. Once you've created a communication starter, test it out at least 5 times on co-workers, friends or family members to see how they respond. Pay attention to their conversational reactions and observe for indicators of rapport. Adjust your communication starter according to how they react to ensure your question is more interesting than small talk.

As you create your communication starter it needs the following elements to create comfort, safety, and trust:

1. Your communication starter has to be in the form of a question, and that question needs to be answerable with more than a yes/no or one word answer – This allows a conversation to develop.

For example: Some good ways to start would be something like:

What do you think about _____?

What is your opinion on _____?

Do you think it's better to be A or B….?

**Example: Do you think it's better to plan for the future or live in the moment?**

2. There has to be a reason for asking the question. The reason makes them feel comfortable. Without a reason, they will feel uncomfortable and start to reject you.

So for example, if your question is:

Do you think it's better to plan for the future or live in the moment?

You could say:

**The reason I ask is because** my friend is refinancing her house. We were talking about disability insurance that would pay her mortgage if she got sick, and she doesn't believe in it. She said: "I like to live in the moment. I don't think about the future." I admired her free spirit and at the same time, I was worried about her. It got me thinking, is it better to plan for the future or live in the moment?

The format to use for your communication starter is:

**The reason I ask is because** _____.

3. There has to be a perceived time limit. When you start talking to a random stranger, they don't know your agenda. They think you want something from them and that makes them nervous or anxious. A time limit alleviates this anxiety by letting them know you're not staying long. So you want to start with a phrase like:

Hey quick question, I'm meeting a client right away, but I could use a fast independent opinion.

4. The question needs to be unique so you're perceived as interesting. Unique – is by comparison to small talk – like the weather, or the hockey game last night etc. The most interesting topics people usually respond to are philosophical in nature, or revolve around relationships between people.

5. "What you ask" has to ignite their curiosity enough that they'll want to give you their opinion. If possible, their opinion should be helpful to you. It feels good when you can help someone and you want to put them in a situation where they feel helpful – so they feel good! The question should not be traumatic; it should be something simple. Trauma does not create comfort, safety or trust.

A trauma example question:

"If you were terminally ill and in lots of pain, do you think it would be better to live in pain, or to partake in assisted suicide?"

That question is too traumatic to start a conversation with, especially with a stranger you're just starting to get to know.

6. What you ask and say should convey something about you in a positive way – this way you stand out form everyone else from the start.

For example:

"Hey quick question, I'm meeting some friends right away, but I could use a fast independent opinion. Do you think it's better to plan for the future or live in the moment? The reason I ask is because my friend is refinancing her house. We were talking about disability insurance that would pay her mortgage if she got sick, and she doesn't believe in it. She said: "I like to live in the moment. I don't think about the future." I admire her free spirit and at the same time, I'm worried about her. It got me thinking, is it better to plan for the future or live in the moment? What do you think?"

The question covey's that you care about your friend.

7. Remember, the communication must start in a way that occurs naturally in the setting you're in. You need to think of your environment and start your conversation the way it would naturally happen there.

For example:

If you're at a coffee shop, people naturally talk to each other in line or waiting for their drink vs. walking up to someone or a group sitting at a table without a coffee in your hand. In line you can start a conversation with the phrase: "While we're waiting in line, let me ask you a quick question..."

That sentence is natural to the environment, and it has a time limit of "while we're waiting in line."

Another one you can use is: Hey real quick, I have to get out of here right away and meet my next client, but let me get your take on something….

Remember you also need to have your own opinion about what you're asking.

The communication starter should not take longer than a minute or two, maybe a bit longer if you're talking to a group of people because they need time to share their answers. Once it's complete, move on. Don't linger on it. Your goal is to successfully start an interesting conversation and begin establishing rapport and then bridge in the direction you want the conversation to go. It is ok if it goes longer than 2 minutes as long as you see the person is engaged and you are observing indicators of rapport. If there is no rapport – wrap it up and bridge in the direction you want to go.

# Exercise 12: Bridging In The Right Direction

1. Memorize the new communication starter you created in the previous exercise.

2. Go somewhere public, like a mall, coffee shop, anywhere there are people you can meet.

3. Mentally state your affirmation or use the following affirmation: "I feel comfortable, honest and trustworthy. This makes me feel excited and grateful because I offer great conversation that helps the people I talk to feel comfortable and have fun!"

4. As soon as you see someone to talk to, silently count to 3, and walk over at an angle, take a breath and say the communication starter you memorized in step 1. It doesn't matter whom you talk to, the idea is to test and practice your communication starter.

5. Observe how the person reacts to your new communication starter and look for indicators of rapport.

6. Once you've listened to the person's opinion, offer your own viewpoint, and say: "It was a pleasure meeting you. Thank you for your help." and turn to walk away. If it's a group of people, get everyone else's opinion before sharing yours.

7. As you take your first step to walk away, turn back and say the following (so you can bridge the conversation in the direction you want it to go)

   - If it's an individual say: "Out of curiosity… What kind of work do you do?"

   - If it's a group of people say: "Out of curiosity… Do you all work together?"

8. Do your best to continue the conversation for at least 2 minutes. You've succeeded when you've bridged the conversation into finding out what kind of work they do. It's a bonus if you get their business card/contact information – if it's appropriate to do so.

9. Repeat this at least 5 times starting with your affirmation and ending your conversation with "It was a pleasure meeting you."

# *Week 5: Uniqueness And Reframing*

What is the law of framing?

_____

_____

_____

Complete the following exercises over the coming week. They are designed for you to break the frame of regular small talk. This way, a person you just met will view you as different and memorable – instead of conforming to their expectations of someone talking about work. These are to be practiced so you develop the skill and have fun.

The idea is to focus on creating a frame of trust, comfort, and safety – so you can overcome or bypass any negative/boring subconscious reactions anyone you speak with might have.

Exercises:

    13. Creating Your Personal Elevator Pitch
    14. A Psychological Game

# Exercise 13: Creating Your Personal Elevator Pitch

1. Complete the Personal Elevator Pitch Creator worksheets on the following pages and memorize the one line pitch you create.

2. Go somewhere public, like a mall, coffee shop, anywhere there are people you can meet. As you've done in past exercises, mentally state your affirmation, comfortably approach the person you want to talk to, start your conversation, and when appropriate – use the following bridge:

   - "Out of curiosity… What kind of work do you do?"

3. Listen to what they do for work, make a positive comment about it, and tell them your one line pitch. Then expand the topic and move the conversation forward. You've succeeded when you've told them about your work. It's a bonus if you get their business card/contact information – where it's appropriate.

4. Repeat this at least 5 times starting with your affirmation and ending your conversation with "It was a pleasure meeting you."

## *Personal Elevator Pitch Creator*

One of the most common questions everyone hears when meeting someone new is:

*"What do you do for a living?*

The purpose of this exercise is to create a one-line description of "what you do" that presents you in an interesting, fun, credible, meaningful and memorable way that is unique to you. How many times have you met someone and they tell you they're a realtor, a car sales man, a banker, a lawyer, an accountant or computer programmer etc., just like every other person in the same position? They present themselves in a boring way and fail to connect with people meaningfully. What's worse – the "label of their occupation" comes loaded with stereotypes, biases, and preconceptions.

Most people give a boring answer because they don't know how to effectively communicate their profession in an interesting and unique way that can lead to better conversation. Answer the following questions and create a succinct and interesting way of answering the question: "What do you do for a living"

1. List the top 3 duties of what you do for a living.

I. _____

II. _____

III. _____

*For example, my personal duties are:*

*I. Speak and perform on stage.*
*II. Consult with clients using mental tools to identify and change detrimental thought patterns to overcome bad habits and improve performance.*
*III. Train clients to increase sales using my unique and successful content.*

2. Who do these duties help?

_____

_____

*My personal example: My duties help sales professionals that want to improve performance and sell more. People that want to overcome bad habits and be more successful. People that want to improve their communication skills in personal and professional areas.*

3. Describe a specific problem people have, that your duties will help a person with?

_____

_____

_____

*My personal example: A sales professional could get a sale, but instead, they get rejected because they don't understand people's subconscious reactions. The sales professional's lack of understanding sabotages safety and trust – and this creates discomfort and rejection in the mind of the prospect.*

4. With regards to this specific problem, what is the most interesting or impactful aspect of what you do for a living that affects people? Does what you do impact everyone? Or a specific group?

_____

_____

_____

_____

_____

_____

*My personal example: Sales professionals can observe and understand the reactions of people and adjust their communication effectively to connect on a meaningful level and convert prospects/clients into buyers and referral partners.*

5. Keeping what you wrote in mind, imagine you are looking to hire someone to manage what you do for a living. Write a headline that would attract a person to this position – a person not involved in what you do, and knows nothing about it. You want to communicate the importance of what you do to them so they understand what they will be doing. Write it in a way that is truthful and communicates to the broadest number of people possible.

Become a manager of _____

_____

(insert title of what you do)

Where you can _____

_____

(insert what you help people with here)

*My personal example: Become a manager of communication, where you can help people increase self-confidence, communicate effectively, and cultivate meaningful relationships.*

Connecting Through Communication
The Art And Science Of Creating Emotionally Intelligent, Genuine Conversations

6. Examine what you wrote and remove unnecessary words that are modifiers (e.g. largest, biggest, fantastic, best etc.). Where you are able to – replace these modifiers with actions words (e.g. create, break, and help etc.). Restate what you wrote above in a simple sentence in under 10 words.

_____

_____

_____

_____

*My personal example: Help people communicate effectively and create meaningful relationships.*

www.ConnectingThroughCommunication.com

© Colin Christopher    77

## Notes

7. Examine what you wrote and ask friends if it is interesting. Are you passionate about the statement? Is it accurate? Does it reflect you? Compare it to the current way you describe what you do. Does it match you? If it does, write your answer to the previous question here starting with the word I:

I... _____

_____

_____

_____

_____

*My personal example: I help people communicate effectively and create meaningful relationships.*

Notes

# Exercise 14: A Psychological Game

1. Memorize the *Triple A's Psychological Connection Game* below.

2. Go somewhere public, like a mall, coffee shop, anywhere there are people you can meet. As in past exercises, mentally state your affirmation, comfortably approach the person you want to talk to, start your conversation, and when appropriate – use the following bridge:

   • Hey… out of curiosity… what kind of work do you do? The reason I ask is because… I heard this fun little psychological test the other day about occupations and how they reveal something about your personality. I'm curious what you think about this: It only takes about 10 seconds: Ok… so, of these three occupations…if you had to pick, which one would you be? An Astronaut, Accountant or Actor/Actress"

3. You've succeeded when you've completed the game and told them what their choice means and shared your choice with them. It's

a bonus if you get their business card/contact information – where appropriate.

4.  Repeat this at least 5 times starting with your affirmation and ending your conversation with "It was a pleasure meeting you."

5.  This exercise is similar to the Elevator Pitch Creator Exercise you did before. The difference will be in how the person reacts in each scenario. It's tempting to skip one of the exercises, but do both. You need to be able to respond in both ways so you can gain the skill of navigating the conversation in the direction you want it to go.

## Triple A's Psychological Connection Game

Take a few minutes and memorize everything in blue, or have the description in your smartphone. The purpose of this game is to create the right opportunity for you to listen and build an emotional connection in an interesting and fun way that sets you apart and allows you to talk about yourself after you've learned something about the person/people you're meeting. This way you connect on a personal level.

Notes

Triple A's works individually, or can be done in a group. In a group, make sure you listen to everyone's answer and focus on them individually so they feel you are listening.

Bridge the conversation.

For example: Hey out of curiosity, what kind of work do you do? The reason I ask is…

Go into the game:

*"I heard this fun little psychological test the other day about occupations and how they reveal something about your personality. I'm curious what you think: It only takes about 10 seconds: Ok… so, of these three occupations…if you had to pick, which one would you be? An Astronaut, Accountant or Actor/Actress" You have 3 seconds… 1, 2, 3!*

Everyone responds one of two ways – They choose one of the 3 or on rare occasions someone will break from the 3 choices, and choose their own.

Which one did you pick? Ok… Here's what that means.

Listen for the answer and give them the description of their personality:

1. Astronaut: A risk taker.
2. Accountant: A person that is happy doing things by the book and likes the rules.
3. Actor/Actress: A person that likes to be the center of things or the life of the party.
4. Their own choice: A person that likes to break the rules and marches to their own beat.

"So is that accurate? Does that describe you?"

Listen to their answer and share your choice. 80% – 85% of the time, what they choose accurately describes them. This allows for an emotional connection because you – a stranger, have given them something very valuable – a fun glimpse into their subconscious. If not accurate – you still have something different to talk about.

Notes

# *Week 6: Uniqueness And Personal Story Telling*

Story telling is a fundamental tool to connect with people. Storytelling is at the core of our being – it's prehistoric communication before the written word was conceived, and it connects us on a primal level. Parents tell their children fairy tales and when you reminisce with friends and family – you share stories. We watch movies and TV because they share stories with us visually. The better the story, the greater the impression, and the more we connect.

When it comes to story telling, many people are terrible storytellers. It's not that they can't tell a story – it's that they go on and on about useless details that are uninteresting and boring. We all know people, who we can't stand because they tell boring stories in irritating ways. And we all know great storytellers that can draw us in, making us want to hear every word.

Stories universally connect us. We all share stories with friends and family and the people we meet everyday. We're all natural storytellers; and when you learn to focus your natural talent for story telling in the right direction, you can use this tool of universal connection and show the people you talk to how unique you are.

The idea behind story telling is to use the story to frame yourself so the people you talk to, and more specifically – their subconscious categorizes you the way you want them to perceive you. That way you can connect with them comfortably. Otherwise their subconscious biases will categorize you based on their past experiences – which may or may not help you – depending on their reaction.

This week you will be working on writing and delivering stories. This process is ongoing as the more stories you create over time, the more opportunities you will have to use them to connect with people. The idea for the following week is to build a solid foundation that you can use as a springboard to develop and master the storytelling skill over time.

For a story to connect with someone, it needs the following components:

1. Make sense in context of the conversation just like your communication starters.
2. The stories have to illustrate something about you.
3. Stories have to give space for the other person/people to respond – again just like your communication starters.

Notes

To develop your personal story telling skills, complete the following exercises:

Exercises:

17. Qualities You Want To Share
18. Write Your Stories
19. Editing, Delivery, Practice, And Evaluation Of Stories
20. Practice Storytelling With Strangers

# Exercise 15: Qualities You Want To Share

1. Make a list of qualities/characteristics that you want people to know about you. Have at least ten. Twenty or more is better. For example: Helpful, funny, thoughtful, etc.

| | |
|---|---|
| 1. _____ | 11. _____ |
| 2. _____ | 12. _____ |
| 3. _____ | 13. _____ |
| 4. _____ | 14. _____ |
| 5. _____ | 15. _____ |
| 6. _____ | 16. _____ |
| 7. _____ | 17. _____ |
| 8. _____ | 18. _____ |
| 9. _____ | 19. _____ |
| 10. _____ | 20. _____ |

2. Choose your top 8 characteristics regarding your work and personal life. Think about your past experiences and identify stories that convey at least 2 or 3 of these characteristics (different stories for different characteristics). The idea is to preselect topics that flow with conversation and communicate your

characteristics. The experiences can be simple, complex, funny or life changing. Here's a list of ideas to get started:

1) Favorite movie
2) Favorite song
3) Favorite sports team
4) Most interesting place you've traveled
5) Favorite hobby
6) The time one of your dreams came true
7) Most interesting place you want to travel
8) Favorite book
9) Favorite meal
10) Favorite band
11) Most interesting work experience
12) Favorite car
13) Most helpful thing anyone's ever done for you
14) Someone you admire
15) Favorite tech gadget
16) Favorite drink
17) Most helpful thing you've done for a client
18) Most interesting thing you've learned about fashion
19) Most interesting thing you've learned about work
20) Most interesting thing you know about the city you live in

# Exercise 16: Write Your Stories

1. Write a title for each story you identified in the last exercise. Following the title, list the characteristics (about you) that each story illustrates. You want to use at least 2 of the characteristics you identified in the first exercise.

2. Write down your stories.

3. After writing your stories, ask yourself the questions below. Depending on your answers, re-write/adjust your stories according to the elements you identify as you answer these questions:

    i. Does this story illustrate the characteristics you want to share?

    ii. Does the story stick to one point or topic? For example: If you're talking about your favourite movie, stick to the movie.

    iii. Are descriptions of items in the story short and easy to follow? Are the details painted in an easy to follow mental picture that moves the story along? Or is there too much detail? Or are there details that are irrelevant to the point or topic of the story.

iv. Is there dialogue? Have dialogue where possible – He said/she said etc. Dialogue is almost always more interesting.

v. Are you using emotionally descriptive words? The more emotional words you use, the better you will connect with people. For example: "I felt great! I was on top of the world!!" is a different picture than "I felt good."

vi. Did you put yourself into the story? When you're in the story, you're sharing a part of you with them. If you're not in the story – how does the story illustrate the characteristics you want to share?

vii. Did you explain why the topic you're talking about is important to you? Did you explain your feelings of the experience?

viii. Is there a moral to the story? What lesson did you learn? Where it's possible and reasonable – include details of yourself that are relevant to your occupation.

ix. Is there humour in the story?

x. Does the story paint you (and the people in it) in a positive way? If it's not positive for everyone involved, consider how the people in the story reflect on you, and revise it so everyone looks good.

xi. Was there anything unexpected that happened? Surprises and twists in the plot make for good stories.

xii. Is there a way to bridge/segue the story into other conversation?

xiii. Is there opportunity for the person you're sharing the story with to ask questions?

It's important to remember: Not every story will conform and include the elements that you're identifying. But the more you include these elements (especially the ones that illustrate the personal characteristics you want to share), the better your stories will be.

Notes

# Exercise 17: Editing, Delivery, Practice, And Evaluation Of Stories

1. After writing your story, leave it for 1-2 days and return to it. Read it and edit it using the following criteria:

    i.   Combine the details of 2 or 3 sentences into 1 sentence where possible. Think and edit with the focus of saying the same thing with less words.

    ii.  Eliminate extra words by shortening sentences.

    iii. Make the language easy to follow by replacing big words – most people speak and comprehend easily at an 8th grade level. The idea is to make it easy for the listener to follow. This also makes it easier for you to remember your story.

    iv.  Examine the language and say the words out loud. Do you talk the same way you write? Adjust the language so the words and order of speech/grammar is the same as when you speak so you sound natural.

    v.   Read the story out loud and record it and see how long it is. Try to get the story length less than 3 minutes. 1 to 2 minutes is preferred. Are there longer stories? Yes.

However, for communicating effectively with someone you've just met, you want to be on point and succinct – so keep the stories short. Longer stories can be used, but they're better used for established relationships (usually).

2. With each story, repeat the first step 2 or 3 more times. Giving yourself time in between allows you to look at your story with fresh eyes.

3. After you've edited 3 to 5 times, break the story up into point form and memorize it (or at least memorize the point form version). This way you can keep yourself on track when you're telling the stories later. In point form include:

   i. Title

   ii. Characteristics of yourself you want to share

   iii. Important details

   iv. Emotions/feelings you want to share

   v. Moral of the story/What you learned

   vi. Anything else you want to include that you find important to remember

vii. You should be able to recite the points in 15 seconds or less.

4. Practice telling the story in front of a mirror and record it so you can listen to how you tell the story. As you tell the stories, vary the speed, pace, and pitch of your voice. Varying the speed makes the listener engage. Monotone voice is very hard to listen to for an extended period of time. How you say anything is just as important as what you say. If you want some examples of how to vary your speed of speech – watch comedians deliver their material and review *Exercise 9: Tone and Speed of Speech* from this program.

5. Enlist the help of a co-worker/friend/family member and explain that you're looking for feedback about some stories you're making to improve your communication. It's good if you do this with more than one person so you can get feedback from multiple people. The more feedback you get, the more you can make a winning story. Before you tell them the story, ask them to pay attention and evaluate so they can answer the following questions about your story:

i. Can they tell what the purpose/topic of the story is?
ii. What qualities about you does the story tell them/illustrate?

iii. Is the story interesting?

iv. Is there anything confusing about the story?

v. Is there anything that should be taken out of the story that's not relevant?

vi. Is there anything that should be added to make the story better?

vii. Do they feel they learned something about you? What did they learn?

6. With your helpers ready to observe the criteria above, share your stories with them, get their feedback, and adjust your stories based on their input.

## Exercise 18: Practice Storytelling With Strangers

1. Go somewhere public, like a mall, coffee shop, anywhere there are people you can meet and start conversations as you've done in the previous exercises. Get yourself to the point in the conversation where you can bridge into your story. A good bridge could be: "Out of curiosity... What's your favourite...?"

i. Start with a question that talks about an experience you've had, or a preference you have. For example: Your favourite movie is a preference. The best vacation you've ever had is an experience. You can ask them: "Out of curiosity, what's your favourite movie?" or "What was your best vacation?"

ii. Listen to their answer.

iii. Bridge and tell your story. You can say something like: "That's a great movie! My favourite movie is…" or if their favourite vacation was Mexico – you could say, "I love Mexico too! My favourite vacation was…"

iv. As you tell your story, explain why you've chosen that experience or preference as your favourite or most interesting. Tell them why it's your favourite movie or best vacation.

v. As you explain why you've chosen that experience or preference – you want to communicate your viewpoint, your thought process, and the personality trait(s) you want to express – to the person you're talking to. Talk about why it's important to you, and talk about the feelings the experience or preference creates within you – what your connection to the story is, and any lesson you learned.

vi. Finish the story with a summary: "That's why my experience/preference is my favourite/most interesting….

vii. At the end of the story – pause and wait for them to respond. You've ended your story in the format of "And that's why X is my favourite Y! For example: And that's why Star Wars is my favourite movie! This creates a natural space for them to speak and respond and it puts the onus on them to continue the conversation.

2. Repeat this at least 5 times with each story you want to use – this is so you can test the story out and see how strangers react. When you consistently get the reactions you want from your story – then you know you've got a good story to share with the people you're talking to.

Here's a sample of one of my stories followed by a breakdown of the elements:

"What's your favourite movie?"

My favourite movie is Star Wars: The Force Awakens

The reason it's my favourite is because I was watching it in the theatre and this girl and her dad were sitting in front of me. I think she was 6 or 7, and we were watching the scene where Rey, the heroine, figures out how to fly the Millennium Falcon.

She said to her dad: "Rey's really good at flying! Do you think I could do that?"

And her dad put his arm around her and said: "Sweetheart, you can do anything you want to, just like Rey!"

He could have easily said, "It's just a movie. It's not real."

For me, I'm always going to think of that movie as a way for a father to connect and encourage his daughter to be anything she can dream of. It gives me faith in humanity that equality is moving forward.

And that's why The Force Awakens is my favourite movie.

_____

In this format I've easily expressed my viewpoints and the traits about myself that I want to communicate by gift-wrapping them inside the experience.

You can see my belief is: Girls (and women for that matter) can be anything they can dream of and I can communicate that viewpoint and connect emotionally to almost any person in about 30 - 45 seconds using that simple story.

Descriptions of items in the story are short so the details paint an easy to follow picture that moves the story along. I was at a movie theatre; the father and daughter were talking in front of me.

You didn't need to know I waited in line for an hour to get into the movie, or the name of my date, or that the little girl was blonde, or the theatre was full, or we were all eating popcorn, or that because I drank too much pop I also had to go to the washroom…

All that detail is irrelevant, yet most people telling a story will include it. Too much detail when talking usually makes stories uninteresting and boring.

Knowing your stories and topics ahead of time, you can eliminate the uninteresting/useless details and focus on how you want to frame yourself in the story – so the people you talk to perceive you in the right way.

Think of it as creating a simple mental picture. Set the scene, tell them what happened, share what you experienced and learned.

Then… end the story.

Keep it simple and short so you can focus on creating comfort, safety and trust.

# *Week 7: Continuation*

1. What is the law of emotional intensity?

_____

_____

_____

_____

2. What is the law of ethics?

_____

_____

_____

Connecting Through Communication
The Art And Science Of Creating Emotionally Intelligent, Genuine Conversations

3. What are the 2 ethical questions to ask yourself when using Connecting Through Communication tools?

1. _____

_____

_____

2. _____

_____

_____

This week you will be working on putting all the skills you've learned together, so you can get the contact information of the people you talk to, and continue the communication into the future. The purpose of communication is so you can create a relationship – when appropriate.

You've done the work and now you're at the stage where the people you're communicating with have subconsciously categorized you as comfortable and safe, and they trust you.

In the process so far, you've just finished sharing a story and/or listening to their story and it's come to a natural conclusion. At that point it's time for you to make a strategic exit. If the conversation is going well, you can certainly stay. But sooner or later the conversation has to end – and you want to get their contact information where appropriate.

You originally started the communication with the a phrase like: "Hey real quick, I'm heading across town right away to meet some friends, but let me get your take on something…"

And so, the natural conclusion to the conversation is:

It's been excellent meeting you and I have to get out of here and meet my friends. You know, you're a really interesting person and it'd be great if we could meet again and talk some more. Let me give you my number…

At this point you can either write your number down or give them your business card. If you write down your number, make sure they write down their number for you, or you get their business card.

## Notes

What works even better is – as you give them your business card, say:

"You know what, why don't you text me quick right now and say:

'It's Astronaut/Accountant/Actress/Actor _____' so I know it's you."

This way, you have their number in your phone right away and the process of being fun and unique carries over in the text message so they remember you too. Plus it seems friendlier than only exchanging business cards. They are usually more likely to continue the conversation if they initiated the text message.

Remember, you are in the drivers seat here. If you've talked to this person and you don't feel they're someone you want to talk to again – Don't exchange contact information! You're not obligated. If you have a negative gut feeling about them, listen to it!

You've been watching them for rapport and have been listening and analyzing their answers to your questions. You've done all this work to ensure that they're comfortable with you, but if you don't feel safe, or comfortable, or you feel you don't trust them – you're probably right.

There is a variation on this if you're at a networking event – You're not going to be using the communication starter: "Hey I have to meet some friends right away, but let me get your take on something…"

You're likely starting the conversation with a quick intro of "who you are" and then going into a question like: "Hey let me get your take on something…" and then going through the process.

So to end the conversation in this scenario and get their contact info you would say:

"It's been excellent meeting you, and I know we're both here to network and meet as many people as we can. I have to say, you're a really interesting person and it'd be great if we could meet again and talk some more. Let me give you my number…"

And from here, exchange info like you did before. Then you're free to continue meeting more people at the networking event.

Once you have their contact information you can continue the conversation either by telephone, and/or set a meeting time and figure out how to further your relationship. You've gotten past the point of starting a new relationship and now you can continue building and moving forward

To continue the communication and create

follow-up opportunities to develop relationships, complete the exercise on the next page.

# Exercise 19: Putting It All Together

1. Go somewhere public, like a mall, coffee shop, anywhere there are people you can meet.

2. Mentally state your affirmation, and as soon as you see someone, walk over and start your communication using the following sentence: "Hey real quick, I'm heading across town right away to meet some friends, but let me get your take on something…" followed by your choice of interesting communication starter questions you developed. Make sure you remember to get and listen to their opinions.

3. Observe for rapport, and bridge from your communication starter into your unique elevator pitch and Triple A's game using the "Out of curiosity… What kind of work do you do?" bridge. Remember to have fun and smile.

4. Continue the conversation bridging into your personal story telling. Use at least one personal story you created. This story frames and conveys (to the person/people you're talking to) one unique quality about you (feel

free to convey more than one quality). Remember to also ask them questions about them, so can you listen and respond to their stories and ensure they are engaging emotionally. For example: You could ask: "What's your favourite movie?" Listen to their answer and then share your favourite movie.

5. Finish the conversation with: "It's been excellent meeting you and I have to get out of here and meet my friends. You know, you're a really interesting person and it'd be great if we could meet again and talk some more. Let me give you my number…"

6. Exchange information and say: "It was a pleasure meeting you. Talk to you soon!" and leave.

7. Once the person is out of visual and auditory range (or when appropriate), write out any notes you need so you can remember the conversation and follow-up/develop the relationship as appropriate.

8. Repeat this at least 5 to 10 times a day for 5 days so you master the skill.

9. Congratulate yourself on a job well done. You earned it!

# *Week 8: Evaluation*

1. What is the law of discipline?

_____

_____

_____

_____

2.  What is the law of will power?

_____

_____

_____

_____

Notes

© Colin Christopher     107

3. What is the law of cumulative contributing factors?

_____

_____

_____

_____

4. What is critical mass? What are you focusing on to achieve it?

_____

_____

_____

_____

Notes

# *Exercise 20: Identifying Areas Of Improvement*

This week you will be evaluating yourself to see how your skills are developing and you'll be identifying areas of improvement. You'll want to do this after every 10 to 20 people you meet so the interactions are still fresh in your mind.

Pull out a notebook, or type on your computer or however you decide to do it. There is also plenty of space after this exercise for writing and evaluating directly in this book.

Thinking about your social interactions from start to finish and answer the following:

1. How many people did you start communication with? How many people did you get contact information for? How many people did you schedule follow-up to further the relationship? Compare these numbers. Are you satisfied with the results? If not, what can you do to improve them?

2. On a scale of 1 to 7, what level of communication anxiety are you experiencing?

3. Based on your communication anxiety number: Is your affirmation helping reduce communication anxiety? If not, is there anything you feel you can do to improve your affirmation?

4. Did the people you started conversations with look comfortable as you walked up to them? Are your angles of approach appropriate?

5. What communication starters did the people you spoke with respond to best?

6. What communication starters did the people you spoke with respond to least?

7. Is there anything you can do to improve your communication starters?

8. What conversation topics did the people you spoke with respond to best?

9. What conversation topics did they respond to least?

10. Is there anything you can do to improve on any of the topics people responded to least? If not, scrap those topics and create better ones.

11. Were there any topics that people you spoke with brought up that seemed engaging and you can do more research on, so you can use it in the future? Write the topics down and schedule a time to research them this week while it's fresh in your mind.

12. Did you use the Triple A's game? How did it go? Are there any areas for improvement?

13. How did people respond to your communication bridges?

14. Did you watch for, and build rapport? Did anything interesting happen in your observations or did anything surprise you?

15. Of the stories that portrayed your best qualities, which one did people respond to best? Which one did they respond to least? Is there anything you can improve that would increase their response to the story? Is there anything that did not go over as you expected? For example: Can you deliver it better? Or memorize it better so you don't forget critical details? Or can you edit the story so it's simpler? If you feel there is nothing that you can change to make a bad story better – drop it and write a new one(s).

16. Did you feel the location you chose to communicate with people was appropriate for meeting the type of people you want to work with? If not, what are the reasons it's not appropriate? Research another location that addresses these reasons and go there next time.

17. Did you exchange contact information? How often?

18. Did you schedule follow-up to develop/further the relationships?

Notes

19. Was there anything that did not go according to plan? Or go as you expected? What was it? What are you doing to create this outcome? What can you do to improve your interactions so they do go as expected?

20. Of the people you met in person, if you did exchange contact information and you're meeting in the future, did you write down what you talked about so you can impress them with remembering their details? Specifically, anything exciting or funny about your meeting, plus their favorite activities, preferences in food, eye color, clothes they were wearing, conversation topics they enjoyed, or any stories they shared? Also, was there a book or something else they recommended, and/or anything else you can build on in future conversation? People are always impressed when you meet them in the future and remember details about them. Remembering makes them feel special and creates emotional entanglement. It also shows you're thoughtful and pay attention to them and makes you unique compared to most other people they've met.

21. Were you fun and interesting? Did you stay fun and interesting throughout the whole interaction process? If not, where did you stop being fun and interesting and what are the reasons? Examine those reasons and decide how to resolve them for next time.

22. Did the people seem comfortable around you? Or were they nervous? What are you doing that creates comfort, safety, and trust?

23. If you're improving communication for work, have you researched other people that are in the same industry to see what they're doing and how you can make yourself unique in comparison?

24. Thinking of all your interactions, were you respectful? Were the people you interacted with respectful? If not, what can you do in the future to ensure mutual respect? Keep in mind, you can't control how other people talk to you, but you can control how you react. If something someone said, or their lack of response creates an emotional reaction in you – it's

your job to identify and resolve that emotion. Are you letting the actions of strangers you've never met influence you? Or are you maintaining your fun and interesting attitude?

25. Think about the qualities you communicated to the people you met through your interesting communication topics and unique stories about yourself. Are there any additional qualities you feel you want to develop that can portray you in a better way to people – so you can connect with them better – especially on an emotional level? Or, if you already have the qualities and haven't come up with appropriate stories – take some time and create stories that illustrate those qualities.

Congratulations! You've made it. Keep up the evaluation process and you'll improve your communications skills very quickly.

Remember – having conversations and communicating should be fun. If you're not having fun, take some time and figure out what will make it fun for you.

Enjoy connecting with people.

Enjoy creating meaningful relationships.

Enjoy your awesome communication skills!

I love hearing about your success. Please remember to share your testimonials with me:

*colin@colinchristopher.com*

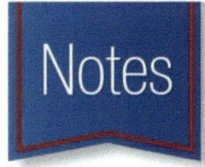

Connecting Through Communication
The Art And Science Of Creating Emotionally
Intelligent, Genuine Conversations

Notes

© Colin Christopher
www.ConnectingThroughCommunication.com

Connecting Through Communication
The Art And Science Of Creating Emotionally
Intelligent, Genuine Conversations

Notes

© Colin Christopher
www.ConnectingThroughCommunication.com

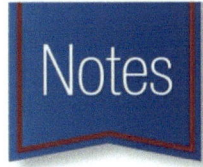

Connecting Through Communication
The Art And Science Of Creating Emotionally
Intelligent, Genuine Conversations

Notes

© Colin Christopher
www.ConnectingThroughCommunication.com

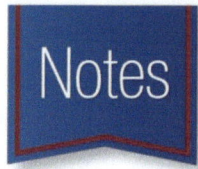

Connecting Through Communication
The Art And Science Of Creating Emotionally
Intelligent, Genuine Conversations

Notes

© Colin Christopher
www.ConnectingThroughCommunication.com

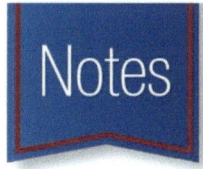

Connecting Through Communication
The Art And Science Of Creating Emotionally
Intelligent, Genuine Conversations

Notes

© Colin Christopher
www.ConnectingThroughCommunication.com

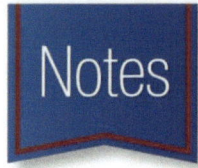

Connecting Through Communication
The Art And Science Of Creating Emotionally
Intelligent, Genuine Conversations

Notes

© Colin Christopher
www.ConnectingThroughCommunication.com

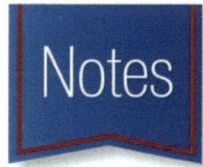

Connecting Through Communication
The Art And Science Of Creating Emotionally
Intelligent, Genuine Conversations

Notes

© Colin Christopher
www.ConnectingThroughCommunication.com

Connecting Through Communication
The Art And Science Of Creating Emotionally
Intelligent, Genuine Conversations

Notes

© Colin Christopher
www.ConnectingThroughCommunication.com

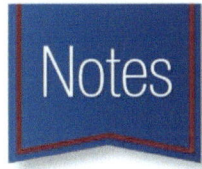

Connecting Through Communication
The Art And Science Of Creating Emotionally
Intelligent, Genuine Conversations

Notes

© Colin Christopher
www.ConnectingThroughCommunication.com

Connecting Through Communication
The Art And Science Of Creating Emotionally
Intelligent, Genuine Conversations

Notes

© Colin Christopher
www.ConnectingThroughCommunication.com

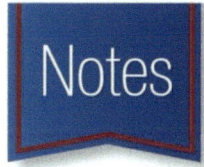

Connecting Through Communication
The Art And Science Of Creating Emotionally
Intelligent, Genuine Conversations

Notes

© Colin Christopher
www.ConnectingThroughCommunication.com

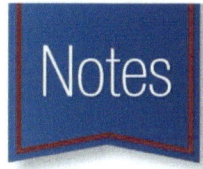

Connecting Through Communication
The Art And Science Of Creating Emotionally
Intelligent, Genuine Conversations

Notes

© Colin Christopher
www.ConnectingThroughCommunication.com

Connecting Through Communication
The Art And Science Of Creating Emotionally
Intelligent, Genuine Conversations

Notes

© Colin Christopher
www.ConnectingThroughCommunication.com

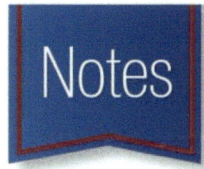

Connecting Through Communication
The Art And Science Of Creating Emotionally
Intelligent, Genuine Conversations

Notes

© Colin Christopher
www.ConnectingThroughCommunication.com

Connecting Through Communication
The Art And Science Of Creating Emotionally
Intelligent, Genuine Conversations

Notes

© Colin Christopher
www.ConnectingThroughCommunication.com

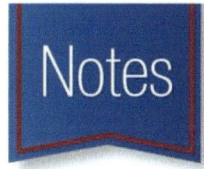

Connecting Through Communication
The Art And Science Of Creating Emotionally
Intelligent, Genuine Conversations

Notes

© Colin Christopher
www.ConnectingThroughCommunication.com

Connecting Through Communication
The Art And Science Of Creating Emotionally
Intelligent, Genuine Conversations

Notes

© Colin Christopher
www.ConnectingThroughCommunication.com

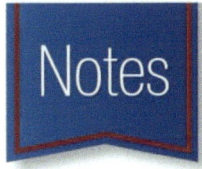

Connecting Through Communication
The Art And Science Of Creating Emotionally
Intelligent, Genuine Conversations

Notes

© Colin Christopher
www.ConnectingThroughCommunication.com

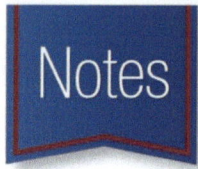

Connecting Through Communication
The Art And Science Of Creating Emotionally
Intelligent, Genuine Conversations

Notes

© Colin Christopher
www.ConnectingThroughCommunication.com

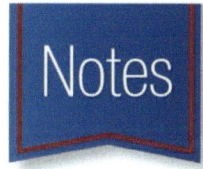

Connecting Through Communication
The Art And Science Of Creating Emotionally
Intelligent, Genuine Conversations

Notes

© Colin Christopher
www.ConnectingThroughCommunication.com

Connecting Through Communication
The Art And Science Of Creating Emotionally
Intelligent, Genuine Conversations

Notes

© Colin Christopher
www.ConnectingThroughCommunication.com

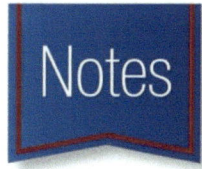

Connecting Through Communication
The Art And Science Of Creating Emotionally
Intelligent, Genuine Conversations

Notes

© Colin Christopher
www.ConnectingThroughCommunication.com

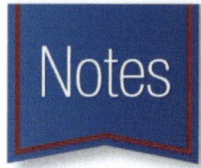

Connecting Through Communication
The Art And Science Of Creating Emotionally
Intelligent, Genuine Conversations

Notes

© Colin Christopher
www.ConnectingThroughCommunication.com

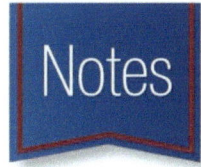

Connecting Through Communication
The Art And Science Of Creating Emotionally
Intelligent, Genuine Conversations

Notes

© Colin Christopher
www.ConnectingThroughCommunication.com

Connecting Through Communication
The Art And Science Of Creating Emotionally
Intelligent, Genuine Conversations

Notes

© Colin Christopher
www.ConnectingThroughCommunication.com

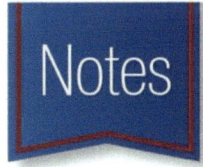

Connecting Through Communication
The Art And Science Of Creating Emotionally
Intelligent, Genuine Conversations

Notes

© Colin Christopher
www.ConnectingThroughCommunication.com

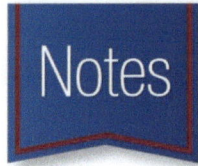

Connecting Through Communication
The Art And Science Of Creating Emotionally
Intelligent, Genuine Conversations

Notes

© Colin Christopher
www.ConnectingThroughCommunication.com

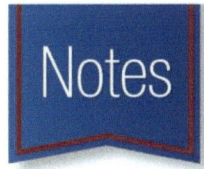

Connecting Through Communication
The Art And Science Of Creating Emotionally
Intelligent, Genuine Conversations

Notes

© Colin Christopher
www.ConnectingThroughCommunication.com

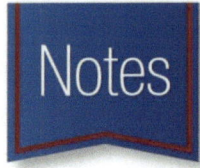

Connecting Through Communication
The Art And Science Of Creating Emotionally
Intelligent, Genuine Conversations

Notes

© Colin Christopher
www.ConnectingThroughCommunication.com

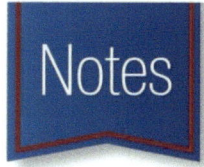

Connecting Through Communication
The Art And Science Of Creating Emotionally
Intelligent, Genuine Conversations

Notes

© Colin Christopher
www.ConnectingThroughCommunication.com

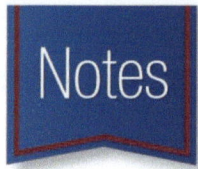

Connecting Through Communication
The Art And Science Of Creating Emotionally
Intelligent, Genuine Conversations

Notes

© Colin Christopher
www.ConnectingThroughCommunication.com

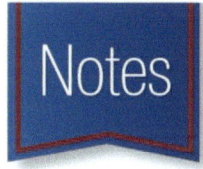

Connecting Through Communication
The Art And Science Of Creating Emotionally
Intelligent, Genuine Conversations

Notes

© Colin Christopher
www.ConnectingThroughCommunication.com

Connecting Through Communication
The Art And Science Of Creating Emotionally
Intelligent, Genuine Conversations

Notes

© Colin Christopher
www.ConnectingThroughCommunication.com

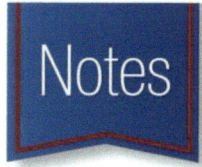

Connecting Through Communication
The Art And Science Of Creating Emotionally
Intelligent, Genuine Conversations

Notes

© Colin Christopher
www.ConnectingThroughCommunication.com

Connecting Through Communication
The Art And Science Of Creating Emotionally
Intelligent, Genuine Conversations

Notes

© Colin Christopher
www.ConnectingThroughCommunication.com

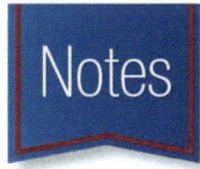

Connecting Through Communication
The Art And Science Of Creating Emotionally
Intelligent, Genuine Conversations

Notes

© Colin Christopher
www.ConnectingThroughCommunication.com

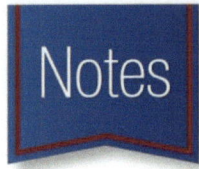

Connecting Through Communication
The Art And Science Of Creating Emotionally
Intelligent, Genuine Conversations

Notes

© Colin Christopher
www.ConnectingThroughCommunication.com

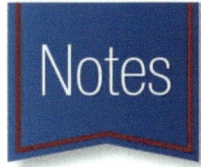

Connecting Through Communication
The Art And Science Of Creating Emotionally
Intelligent, Genuine Conversations

Notes

© Colin Christopher
www.ConnectingThroughCommunication.com

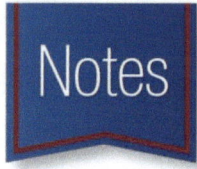

Connecting Through Communication
The Art And Science Of Creating Emotionally
Intelligent, Genuine Conversations

Notes

© Colin Christopher
www.ConnectingThroughCommunication.com

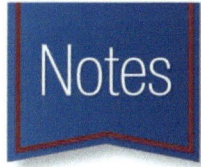

Connecting Through Communication
The Art And Science Of Creating Emotionally
Intelligent, Genuine Conversations

Notes

© Colin Christopher
www.ConnectingThroughCommunication.com

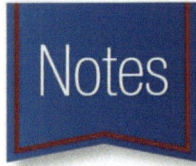

Connecting Through Communication
The Art And Science Of Creating Emotionally
Intelligent, Genuine Conversations

Notes

© Colin Christopher
www.ConnectingThroughCommunication.com

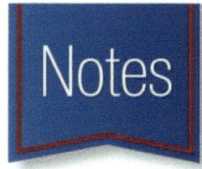

Connecting Through Communication
The Art And Science Of Creating Emotionally
Intelligent, Genuine Conversations

Notes

© Colin Christopher
www.ConnectingThroughCommunication.com

Connecting Through Communication
The Art And Science Of Creating Emotionally
Intelligent, Genuine Conversations

Notes

© Colin Christopher
www.ConnectingThroughCommunication.com

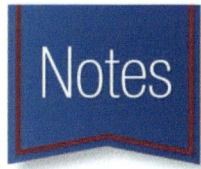

Connecting Through Communication
The Art And Science Of Creating Emotionally
Intelligent, Genuine Conversations

Notes

© Colin Christopher
www.ConnectingThroughCommunication.com

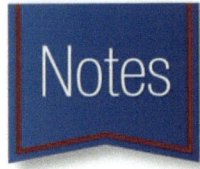

Connecting Through Communication
The Art And Science Of Creating Emotionally
Intelligent, Genuine Conversations

Notes

© Colin Christopher
www.ConnectingThroughCommunication.com

# *Learning Resources*

**Sales Training**
http://www.manipulatethesale.com/

**Colin's TV Interviews and featured articles:**
http://www.colinontv.com/

**Sales Training**
http://www.manipulatethesale.com/

**Success Through Manipulation Book:**
http://www.successthroughmanipulationbook.com/

**Manipulate The Date Book:**
http://www.manipulatethedate.com/

**Free Weight Loss Program Using Hypnosis:**
http://www.freeloseweighthypnosis.com/

**Always Afraid? Conquer Your Fear Using Hypnosis:**
http://www.alwaysafraid.com/

**Hypnosis for Child Birth:**
http://www.easybabybirth.com/

**Hypnosis Health Store:**
http://www.hypnosishealthstore.com/

**Free Hypnotist Course:**
http://www.freehypnotistcourse.com/

**Colin Christopher's Official Hypnosis Site:**
http://www.colinchristopher.com/

**Colin Christopher's Success Through Manipulation Speaking Site:**
http://www.successthroughmanipulation.com/
**Facebook:**
http://www.facebook.com/colinchristopher/

**Twitter:**
http://www.twitter.com/colinontv/

**Instagram:**
http://www.instagram.com/colinchristopherspeaks/

**LinkedIn:**
http://www.linkedin.com/in/colinchristopher/

# COLIN CHRISTOPHER

www.colinontv.com · Phone: 780-903-1677 · Email: colin@colinchristopher.com

# MANIPULATE THE SALE

## PSYCHOLOGICAL TOOLS THAT SELL MORE

Manipulate The Sale trains people how the conscious and subconscious minds of buyers and sellers influence communication and sales. As you learn the psychological tools that sell more, you will be able to apply them to prospecting, client relationship building, and creating referral opportunities, so you can:

- ✔ Book more appointments
- ✔ Close more sales
- ✔ Earn more money
- ✔ Build instant rapport
- ✔ Make your prospects and clients quickly comfortable
- ✔ Capture attention and make people ask for more

- ✔ Create lasting meaningful connections
- ✔ Make yourself a socially valuable leader
- ✔ Gain peace of mind
- ✔ Have more fun and genuinely be more successful
- ✔ Standout from the competition
- ✔ Become a sales champion

| INCREASE SALES | IMPROVE COMMUNICATION | MANAGE SUCCESS |
|---|---|---|

## Interactive Online Sales Training

Colin Christopher discuses and provides psychological tools designed to communicate effectively with prospects, clients, and referral partners. You will learn to create comfort, safety, trust, and loyalty in the mind of your buyers, so that you sell more.

www.manipulatethesale.com

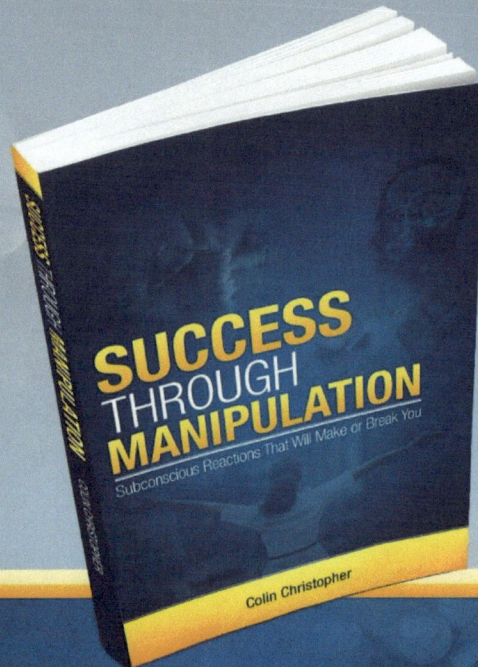

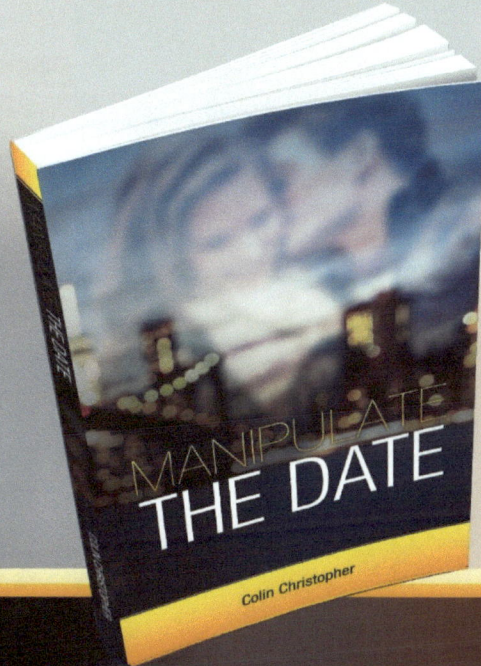

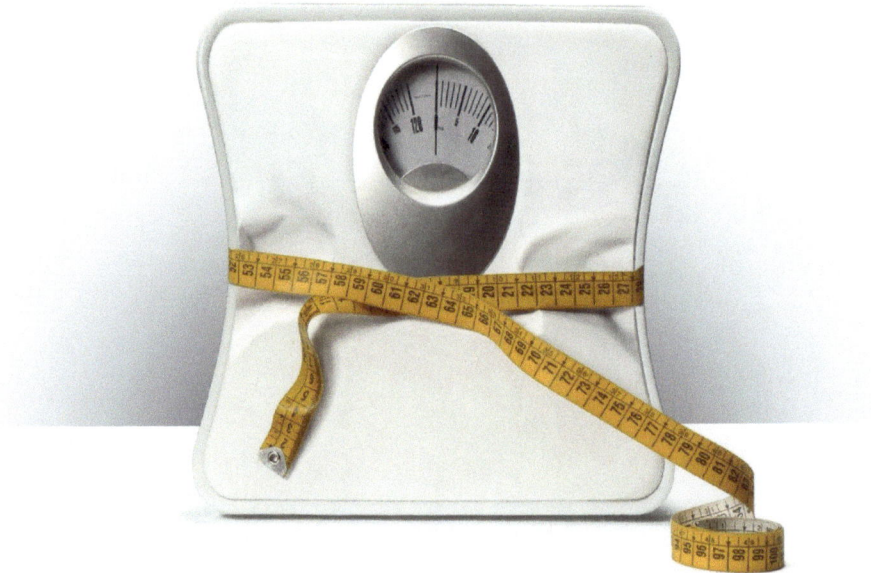

# LOSE WEIGHT WITH HYPNOSIS FOR FREE

In the news today, they say obesity is an epidemic. If this is true for you and you want to lose weight, there is help. And it's FREE.

When it comes to weight, lighter people think differently than heavier people. Because they think differently, lighter people don't have the mental barriers that heavier people do.

Using this FREE hypnosis program, you're going to put your mind and body into a relaxed state. Then you're going to train your subconscious mind to think like lighter people do. That way you can break through the mental barriers that are keeping you heavy!

## www.freeloseweighthypnosis.com

# ALWAYS AFRAID?
# CONQUER YOUR FEAR!

Does Fear hold you back?  Do you have anxiety?
Phobia's get you down?

| | |
|---|---|
| Stage Fright? | Bees? |
| Snakes? | Anxiety? |
| Spiders? | Phobia? |

What are you afraid of?

There is help.  You're not alone.

Ever wonder why you're afraid of something and someone else isn't?  It's because they react differently than you do.  Change how you react so you are comfortable and calm.

Using this hypnosis program, you're going to put your mind and body into a relaxed state to train your subconscious mind and change your fight or flight response.  That way you can break through the mental barriers that makeyou afraid!

Try it.  It's safe.  It's relaxing.  You have nothing to fear but fear itself!

## www.alwaysafraid.com

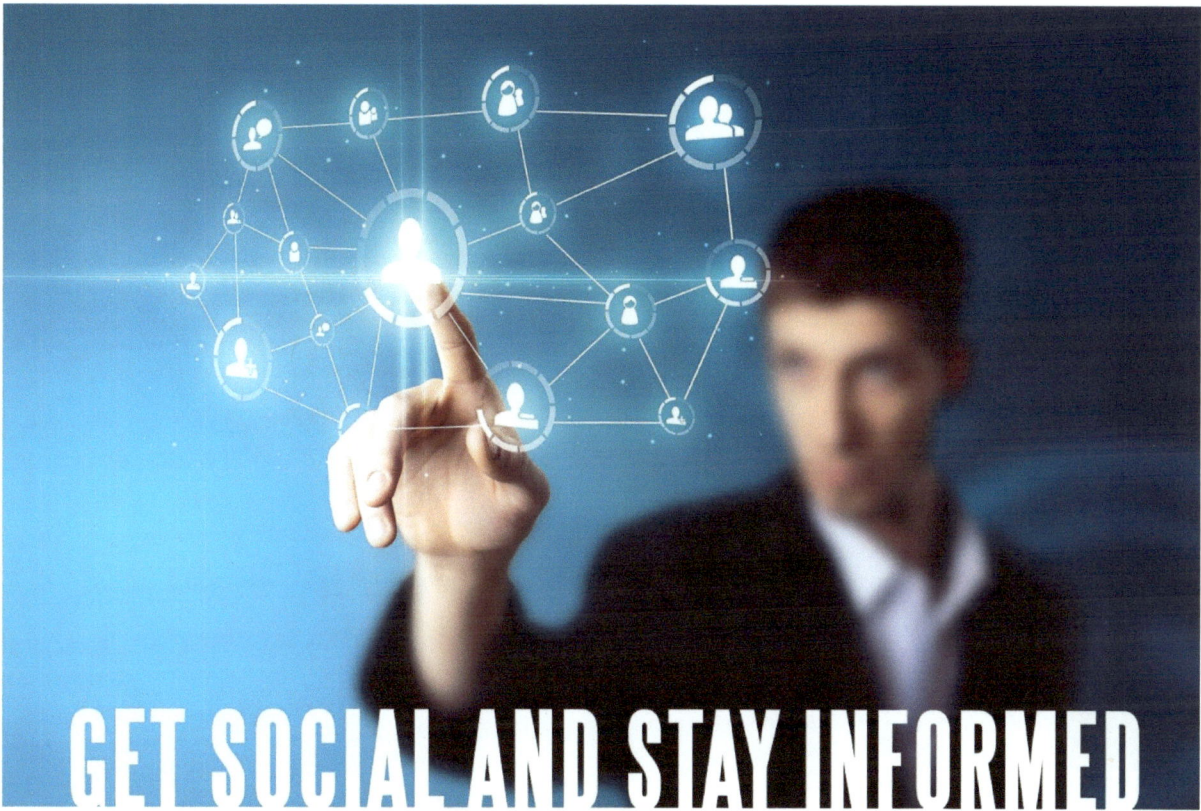

**GET SOCIAL AND STAY INFORMED**

Facebook:

www.facebook.com/colinchristopher/

Twitter:

www.twitter.com/colinontv/

LinkedIn:

www.linkedin.com/in/colinchristopher/

# About The Author

Colin Christopher is a keynote speaker, stage hypnotist and sought after authority in hypnosis appearing all over the world on networks like **ABC, CBS, NBC, FOX, ESPN, Global, City, CTV,** and many others.

As a clinical hypnotherapist, hypnosis instructor, and author, Colin has also been featured in hundreds of prominent publications like the **LA Times, Daily Mail UK, Metro New York, ELLE,** and **Psychology Today**.

Visit **http://www.colinontv.com** and watch TV interviews and read many of his feature articles.

Some of his clients include **Lexus, Chevrolet, Buick, GMC, Staples, McDonalds, Bell Mobility, CIBC, TD Trust, BMO, Husky Energy, Ernst & Young, Celebrity Cruise Lines,** and **Princess Cruise Lines**.

As a thought leader, he's shared his unique take on hypnosis and manipulation while sharing stages with world-class celebrity speakers like **Bob Proctor, Steve Siebold,** and **Brian Tracy**.

Off stage, Colin is a clinical hypnotherapist, hypnosis instructor and author of the books:

- ***Success Through Manipulation***
- ***Manipulate The Date***
- ***Manipulate The Weight***
- ***Manipulate The Sale***
- ***Connecting Through Communication***

Visit Colin's websites to learn more about his one of a kind perspective on thought manipulation and success.